131 Conversations That Engage Kids

How to Get Kids Talking, Grow Their Friendships, and Inspire Change

Jed Jurchenko

www.CoffeeShopConversations.com

Printed by CreateSpace,
An Amazon.com Company
Available from Amazon.com

Dedicated to parents, stepparents, foster parents, teachers, mentors, and coaches who tirelessly build into the lives of kids.

Dedicated to the children and tweens striving to build face-to-face connections in an increasingly virtual world.

Dedicated to my own children, Mackenzie, Brooklyn, Addison, and Emmalynn.
May your contagious joy, compassion for others, and desire to be good friends, continue to grow!

Bonus Gift #1

To thank you for your purchase, I would like to send you two bonus gifts.

Transform from discouraged and burned out, to an enthusiastic agent of joy who leads at a higher–happier–level! *Be Happier Now*, is easy to apply and is perfect for parents, mentors, ministers, business leaders, and friends.

www.coffeeshopconversations.com/happiness/

Bonus Gift #2

In addition, I will send you *The Ultimate Happiness Checklist PDF*!

Discover the ten happiness principles in *Be Happier Now*, in an easy to digest format. This simple tool provides insights into why your happiness matters to everyone around you. It will motivate you to continue your happiness journey by applying what you have learned!

www.coffeeshopconversations.com/happiness/

Contents

Bonus Gifts..4

***

The Big Deal About Small Talk........................9

131 Conversations That Engage Kids...........23

Connecting in a Disconnected World...........49

***

End Notes..52

Thumbs Up or Down.......................................54

About the Author..56

More Creative Conversations.........................58

The Big Deal
About Small Talk

Welcome to *131 Conversations That Engage Kids*, a small book with the big goal of getting kids talking and keeping them engaged. This book is for two primary audiences. First, it is for adults who want to help children build strong connections in an increasingly virtual and disconnected world. This includes parents, stepparents, foster parents, teachers, coaches, youth pastors, and mentors. Second, this book is for children and tweens longing to build face-to-face friendships that develop into life-long bonds.

There are four important reasons for getting intentional about face-to-face conversation. First, conversations create connection. Second, they influence positive life change. Third, conversations build social skills, and fourth, they are a whole lot of fun. The conversation starters in this book are practically guaranteed to get your kids talking and keep them engaged. However, before diving in, let's first examine why each of these areas is so important!

Goal #1: Talking to Connect

Conversation is one of the primary ways that people connect. This is true for both children and adults. Psychology uses the term *attachment,* to describe the close bonding that takes place among family members and friends. Multiple studies have concluded that a secure attachment results in lower levels of anxiety, depression, and worry. It also leads to increased levels of success in college and better interpersonal relationships throughout one's lifetime.[1] In this book, the words *attachment* and *connection* are used interchangeably. Connection is important because, as students of human behavior know, connection changes everything!

The Connection Advantage

Connection is what allows a petite, five-foot mother to keep her six-foot tall, athletic son in check. When the teenage years arrive, physically enforcing rules at home becomes increasingly difficult. One does not simply pick-up a teenager and set him or her on time-out, and attempting to do so would be foolish. Placing incessant restrictions on beloved items such as cell phones, extracurricular activities, and household privileges is exhausting. Fortunately, a strong bond between parent and child can render these methods unnecessary. I am acquainted with a number of teens who follow the rules, not because they have to, nor because they want to, but because they cannot stand the thought of breaking their mom or dad's heart.

A strong attachment is what causes friends and family to stick together through thick and thin. It is also the reason why sports teams give 110%. When children are connected, they push themselves over, above, and beyond what they feel capable of accomplishing, because when someone we are connected to believes that we are capable, we believe it too. In short, attachment is the foundation of multiple types of success.

Attachment Metaphors

There are two excellent metaphors for attachment. First, attachment is an invisible string that crosses cities, states, oceans, and continents. This unseen bond allows children to feel loved, even when they are a great distance away.

Second, a strong attachment is like a revitalizing well of water in the midst of a scorching wasteland. Kind words submerge themselves deep into our children's hearts and are later drawn upon for strength and comfort. Object relation therapists use the word introjection to describe the internal connection to others that continues throughout life.

Connection and Intimacy

Although nearly everyone longs for close connections, not everyone knows how to cultivate them. A sunflower requires water, oxygen, sunlight, rich soil, and time in order to blossom. Similarly, positive attachments require time, consistency, and mutual intimacy.

Although intimacy is an odd term for a book for preteens, our definition fits nicely. In this book, intimacy is defined as in-to-me-see. It is the act of allowing another person to peer into one's inner world while simultaneously sharing one's own heart. Intimacy covers the entire gambit of a person's inner life by starting shallow and deepening over time. Attachment begins with face-to-face conversation, and is the glue that binds people together through all of the ups and downs of life.

For preteens, having safe adults and positive peers to share their inner world with is especially important. As we will see in this next goal, the people our children are closest to, have a big part in steering which direction they will go.

Goal #2: Talking for Change

Conversation is a key that unlocks positive life change and dynamic personal growth. Although the conversations in this book do not push for change directly, they do create an environment where growth is possible. Let me explain with a simple illustration. A car cruising down the highway in the wrong direction can easily get back on track with a few turns of the steering wheel. On the other hand, a car stuck in the mud, or at a broken standstill, requires a great deal effort to reach its destination—even if that car is pointed in the right direction.

Similarly, preteens, who are actively engaged in conversations with positive adults can be gently guided in the right direction. On the other hand, supporting youth who are checked-out is a daunting task. I know this from years of personal experience. Crossed arms, avoidance of eye contact, and a glazed-over look are barriers to growth that no amount of logic, lectures, or life-wisdom will penetrate. Reengagement is required first. Then, and only then, can growth occur. This book is about "fueling the car," so that you can steer the conversation where it needs to go.

If you already have engaged kids and want to take the next steps, be sure to check out my book, *131 Creative Conversations for Families*. This resource hones-in on value-based conversations that promote wisdom and maturity in thirteen different areas of life. However, because these conversations focus on growth and not engagement, it is a good idea to start with the conversations in this book, and to deepen your dialogue over time.

Goal #3: Conversation Build Social Skills

Basic social skills are no longer as basic as they once were, and many are becoming a lost art. Virtual relationships via text, e-mail, and social media are the new norm. Parents who spent their childhood playing dress-up with friends, creating imaginary worlds, and having outdoor adventures until the streetlights came on bemoan how their preteens gather together, only to zone-out in front of their electronic devices.

Today's kids are simultaneously more connected and more disconnected than any prior generation. Long-distance friendships come easily, while face-to-face connections can be scary. The conversation starters in this book provide the opportunity to practice the communication skills that do not come as naturally to the electronically savvy. Here are five, key conversational micro-skills to reinforce while going though this book:

1. Gentle Eye Contact:

It is said, the eyes are the window to the soul. Eye contact nonverbally communicates, "You are important." One's gaze should be confidant, warm, and natural. Finding that balance between lazar-intensity and distracted wandering comes with practice.

2. Keep an Open Posture:

It is estimated that as much as 93% of communication is non-verbal.[2] Communicate warmth and interest by keeping an open posture. Turn your body toward the other person, with arms and legs uncrossed. This simple gesture says, "I am open to hearing what you have to say."

3. Listen Actively:

Active listening involves drawing out the speaker's story with simple affirmations. This includes head-nods, a soft smile, and verbal "uh-hu's," that inform the speaker that you are tracking with what is said.

4. Appreciate Differences:

Face-to-face conversations are the perfect time to practice appreciating differences. If you and your friend were alike in every way, then one of you would not be necessary. It is entirely possible to listen empathetically and considerately even if you do not agree with every point made. Knowing how to listen to a variety of opinions in a respectful manner is an exceptionally valuable skill to master.

5. Draw the Speaker Out:

Finally, draw the speaker out with good follow up questions. Do not just act interested, be interested. The easiest way to accomplish this is to get curious about the other person's perspective. Everyone has unique life experiences from which we can learn. Our job is to draw their story out.

Goal #4: Talking for Fun

Finally, talking is fun, and having fun is a big deal. In fact, it is so important that the renowned therapist, William Glasser, the founder of choice theory, considered it one of the five basic, human needs. Fun matters for at least three reasons.

First, children mature through play and fun. Second, fun is a stress reliever that greatly benefits our mental health. The diathesis-stress model of mental illness suggests that high levels of stress increase the chance of mental illness. This means that having fun may keep you from driving yourself crazy—literally! Finally, as you probably already know, fun is a powerful relationship builder. Fun times create fantastic memories, which lead to lasting friendships.

Appropriate humor and a playful attitude are powerful allies in nearly every area of life. If you are not having fun, then you are doing things wrong. Although the conversations in this book are designed to be fun, funny, interesting, and highly engaging, here are some additional strategies for getting the most out of the pages ahead:

1. Conversation Jenga

Purchase a Jenga game (or a similar type of block stacking game), if you do not own one already. Using a marker, write a number on each block (or write the numbers on small stickers and attach them to each block). Next, build the tower and follow the usual instructions, with one simple twist. After each person removes a block from the tower, that person must answer the question that corresponds to the number on his or her block.

2. Conversation Beach Ball

Inflate a beach ball, and using a permanent marker, write the numbers 1-131 on the ball. The position of the numbers on the ball is unimportant, so long as the numbers cover a large portion of the ball's surface. To start the game, toss the beach ball to a family member or friend. The person who catches the ball must locate the number closet to his or her right thumb and answer the corresponding question in this book. Then, he or she should toss the ball to the next player.

3. Conversation Balloon Pop

This icebreaker is perfect for parties and high-energy engagement. Either make copies of your favorite questions or write the number of those questions on a thin strip of paper. Next, place each strip of paper inside of a separate balloon and inflate. Have fun bouncing the balloons back and forth, mixing up the conversation starters. Then, take turns popping the balloons and answering the questions inside.

Other strategies for getting the most out of this book include going through the questions over dinner or before bedtime (which is often one of the easiest times to get a conversation going). You could also store this book in the car for use on road trips or use it consistently during the daily drive to school.

The most important thing is to take pleasure in the process. This book is not a task to complete, but a journey to be enjoyed. There is no prize for finishing every question, no time-line, no penalty for skipping over conversation starters that don't resonate with you, and nothing miraculous happens when the book is complete. The real magic is in the process itself. So take your time and have fun, every step of the way!

Sincerely,

COFFEE SHOP CONVERSATIONS

131
Conversations That Engage Kids

*While we try to teach our children
all about life, Our children teach us
what life is all about.*

~ Angela Schwindt, home schooling mom

*Children are great imitators.
So give them something great to imitate.*

~ Anonymous

Conversation #1

If you were president of the United States, what is one law that you would enact or change?

Conversation #2

If you took a sneak peek at Santa's list, do you think that you would find your name on the naughty or nice list, and Why?

Conversation #3

If you had the opportunity to ask God a single question, what would it be?

Conversation #4

Which of *The Seven Dwarfs* best describes you today?–Bashful, Dopey, Sleepy, Sneezy, Grumpy, Happy, or Doc.

Conversation #5

If you could travel back in time and spend the day with one historical figure, who would it be and why?

Conversation #6

What is one book that you believe every child should read?

Conversation #7

If you had to choose one food to eat every single day for the next year, what would it be?

Conversation #8

In the book *Wonder*, Mr. Browne's precept for the month of October states, "Your deeds are your monuments." What is one of your monuments that makes you especially proud?

Conversation #9

If you took the place of the girl Riley Anderson in the cartoon *Inside Out*, which emotion would be at your controls most often–Joy, Sadness, Fear, Disgust, or Anger?

Conversation #10

If you had to choose between going through the rest of your life not being able to see or not being able to hear, which would you choose, and why?

Conversation #11

If you could have any superpower what would it be, and how would you use this skill for good?

Conversation #12

What is one, simple pleasure, that made you happy today?

Conversation #13

If the zoo offered to let you keep an exotic animal as a pet, what animal would you bring home with you?

Conversation #14

What is the kindest thing that someone has done for you this week?

Conversation #15

How have you been kind to someone else this week?

Conversation #16

An old precept says, "It is better to give than to receive." Do you believe this statement is true? Why, or why not?

Conversation #17

How do people know when they are in love? When you fall in love, how will you know?

Conversation #18

Some people make a "bucket list," or a list of things they hope to do and see before they die. What are two things that you would put on your bucket list?

Conversation #19

In the book *The Adventures of Tom Sawyer*, Tom and his friend Huck Finn sneak into their own funeral and listen to their eulogies. Imagine that, like Tom and Huck, you have the opportunity to listen in at your own funeral. What do you hope your friends and family say about you?

Conversation #20

If you had the opportunity to give one piece of advice to our current president, what would it be?

Conversation #21

What do you think happens to people immediately after they die?

Conversation #22

If you inherited Superman's ability to fly for a single day—and only for one day—where would you go and what would you do?

Conversation #23

In the movie *Frozen*, Elsa has power over ice and snow. Instead of embracing this gift, she conceals it, because she is different. What makes you feel different from others and causes you to want to hide?

Conversation #24

What song makes you want to dance the most?

Conversation #25

When was the last time that you said the words, "I'm sorry," and what did you apologize for?

Conversation #26

What family member do you look up to, and what specifically do you admire about this person?

Conversation #27

Finish this sentence: "The best part about being me is..."

Conversation #28

Complete this sentence: "Something difficult about being me is..."

Conversation #29

Imagine that you have the ability grant your parents one superpower. What superhuman ability will you bestow upon them, and why?

Conversation #30

What is one thing that you admire about your mom or dad?

Conversation #31

What is one thing that your mom or dad say that they appreciate about you?

Conversation #32

If you were asked to choose the next president of the United States, who would you appoint to run the country, and why?

Conversation #33

What cartoon character has a personality most like your own?

Conversation #34

Complete this sentence: "One food I would be perfectly happy never eating again is..."

Conversation #35

If you had to go through the rest of your life with either no arms or no legs which would you choose? Why?

Conversation #36

Imagine that a genie offers to grant you a single wish, and wishing for more wishes is forbidden. What would your wish be?

Conversation #37

In the movie *Freaky Friday*, a mom and daughter switch bodies for a day. If you woke up in your mom or dad's body, how would you spend the day?

Conversation #38

If Santa Clause offered to give you an early Christmas present—one that you would receive this very moment—what would you ask for?

Conversation #39

Finish this sentence, "One lesson I learned, or am learning, this year is..."

The only man who never makes a mistake is the man who never does anything.
~Theodore Roosevelt

Conversation #40

Imagine that a rich relative passes away and leaves you in charge of managing his estate. Your first task is to donate one million dollars of his money to any charity or worthy cause you choose. How would you use this money to help others?

Conversation #41

Imagine this rich relative gave you a million dollars to spend any way you like. What is the first purchase that you would make for yourself?

Conversation #42

If you could change one rule in your home, what would it be, and why?

Conversation #43

What is a rule in your home that you appreciate, and why do you like this rule?

Conversation #44

Imagine a famous movie producer wants to make a major motion picture about your life. You get to select a Hollywood star to play you. Whom would you choose, and why?

Conversation #45

What is something that brought you joy this week?

Conversation #46

The word *phobia,* is used to describe irrational fears. Some people are terrified of spiders (arachnophobia), others are afraid of heights (acrophobia), or panic when confined to a small space, like an elevator (claustrophobia). What irrational fear might you possess?

Conversation #47

Who is one of your best friends and what is one thing that you admire about this person?

Conversation #48

What is one thing that happened this week that was frustrating or annoying? (Even small frustrations count.)

Conversation #49

Describe a favorite holiday memory. Where did you go, what did you do, and why was this time so meaningful for you?

Conversation #50

Complete this sentence: "The most adventurous thing I did this year was..."

Conversation #51

Finish this sentence: "An injustice in our world that makes me mad is..."

Conversation #52

If you could pick a famous person to mentor you for a day–such as a well-known athlete, musician, artist, writer, etc,–who would you choose, and what would you ask them to teach you?

Conversation #53

Finish this sentence: "The most stressful part of being me is..."

Conversation #54

When you are feeling sad, mad, or frustrated, what activity makes you smile again.

Conversation #55

Complete this sentence, "The best part about being me is..."

Conversation #56

If you were principal of your school for a day, what is one school rule that you would change?

Conversation #57

An old adage says, "Children should be seen but not heard." Do you agree or disagree with this statement, and why?

Conversation #58

Who is the bravest person you know? What do you think it is that makes this person so brave?

Conversation #59

Name one movie that you think everyone ought to see. Then, explain why people need to watch this movie.

Conversation #60

Walt Disney said, "If you can dream it, you can do it." If you knew, without a doubt, that you could do anything and would not fail, what would you do?

Conversation #61

In the movie *Rockey*, Rockey Balboa, has a theme song that makes him feel powerful when he trains for upcoming boxing matches. What song gets you motivated and energized?

Conversation #62

An extrovert feels energized when he or she is around people. An introvert is refreshed by spending time alone. Do you think that you are more of an extrovert or an introvert?

Conversation #63

If you had to choose one sport—and only one sport—to watch for the rest of your life, what would it be?

Conversation #64

Imagine that your parents tell you it is time to look for a part-time job. Where would enjoy working, and why?

Conversation #65
Finish this sentence: "A job I hope to never work, under any circumstances is..."

Conversation #66
Name three qualities you possess that make you a good friend?

Conversation #67
Imagine that you wake up this Monday and discover that school is canceled. How would you want to spend your day?

Conversation #68
What is your favorite subject in school, and why?

Conversation #69
What is your least favorite subject in school, and why?

Conversation #70
Imagine a rich relative offers to buy you your first car—absolutely any car you choose. What vehicle would you ask for?

Conversation #71

In the Harry Potter series, certain wizards know as animagus, have the ability to transform into animals. If you were an animagus, what animal would you change into, and how would you use your power?

Conversation #72

A pet peeve is a little irritation—like biting one's fingernails or burping after a meal—that you find especially annoying. What is one of your biggest pet peeves?

Conversation #73

Sometimes adults like to say, "A penny saved is a penny earned?" Do you believe this statement is true, and that saving money is the same as earning money? Why?

Conversation #74

Imagine your birthday is declared a national holiday, like Thanksgiving, Christmas, or Presidents Day. Describe how you would like people to celebrate your holiday?

Conversation #75

Steve Jobs, the former CEO of Apple Inc. recalls being asked by his fourth grade teacher, "What is it that you don't understand about the universe?"[3] How would you answer this question?

Conversation #76

Your house is on fire! Fortunately, your family and pets are safe. Unfortunately, you only have time to grab three personal belongings before scrambling outside. What will you take with you?

Conversation #77

You can choose any musical group to play at your birthday party this year. What band do you pick and what opening song will they play?

Conversation #78

Imagine that you are given the task of abolishing one holiday—meaning no one will be allowed to celebrate this holiday ever again, in any way, shape, or form. Which holiday will you eliminate?

Conversation #79

What is your favorite holiday, and how do you celebrate it?

Conversation #80

What is your favorite comfort food to enjoy after a stressful day? When was the last time you ate it?

Conversation #81

Surprise, you get to choose your own allergies. What two foods will you be allergic to for the rest of your life?

Conversation #82

Today everyone will call you by your favorite nickname. How will everyone refer to you?

Conversation #83

Complete this sentence: One app, video game, or computer program I cannot do without is...

Children see magic because they look for it.
~ Christopher Moore, writer

Conversation #84

When you get in trouble, would you rather be put on phone restriction, television restriction, or internet restriction, and why?

Conversation #85

Finish this sentence: An unusual talent I have is...

Conversation #86

Tell a story about a time you were embarrassed. Who was involved and what happened?

Conversation #87

If you could travel back in time and give one piece of advice to your younger self, what advice would you give?

Conversation #88

Finish this sentence. "Parents should always..."

Conversation #89

Finish this sentence. "Parents should never..."

Conversation #90

If you could spend the day binge watching any television series, what show would you watch?

Conversation #91

What movie do you hope they make a sequel to soon?

Conversation #92

What movie is so bad that it should never, under any circumstances, have a sequel made?

Conversation #93

Tomorrow, you have the option of going skydiving, scuba diving, or staying home and watching television. What activity would you choose, and why?

Conversation #94

Surprise, you get to compete on any game show you want! Which one will you choose, and why?

Conversation #95

What bad habit are you currently trying to break?

Conversation #96

What is one good and healthy habit that you have?

Conversation #97

You are about to be stranded on a tropical island for a year and get to take one luxury item with you. What will you bring, and why?

Conversation #98

You are about to be stranded on a deserted island for a year and get to bring one music album with you. What album will you take?

Conversation #99

You are about to be stranded on a deserted island for a year and get to bring one—and only one—book with you. Which book will you choose?

Conversation #100

The elf on the shelf came early this year and has been watching you all week long. Now he is reporting back to Santa. Describe a high point of the week that Santa will hear about.

Conversation #101

The elf on the shelf came early this year and has been watching you all week. Now he is reporting back to Santa. This time, describe a low point of the week that Santa will hear about.

Conversation #102

No two snowflakes are exactly alike. No two people are the same either. What is something that makes you unique or special?

Conversation #103

Do you usually remember your dreams or forget them? If your remember them, describe one dream that you are able to recall.

Conversation #104

Describe a favorite family holiday tradition.

Conversation #105

Describe an all-time favorite Halloween costume. What did you dress up as, why did you like this costume, and how did others react to it?

Conversation #106
Describe a happy memory from a favorite family vacation.

Conversation #107
Finish this sentence: "The world would be a better place if..."

Conversation #108
Complete this phrase: "Something many people don't know about me is..."

Conversation #109
If your life was turned into a book, what would the title of your story be?

Conversation #110
If your life was turned into a book, where in the bookstore would it be found, (drama, comedy, adventure, romance, suspense, etc.) and why?

Conversation #111
What was the worst injury you ever had, and how did it happen?

Conversation #112

Imagine that you peer into a crystal ball that allows you to peek ten years into the future. Describe what you see.

Conversation #113

In your opinion, what is the perfect combination of pizza toppings?

Conversation #114

In your opinion, at what age should children have privilege and responsibility of a smartphone, and why?

Conversation #115

In your opinion, what flavor of ice cream should never be invented?

Conversation #116

If you could visit any country in the world, which country would it be? Why?

Conversation #117

Which pieces of Halloween candy do you always eat first?

Conversation #118

What is one thing that you did in the last month to make this world a better place? (Even little acts are OK).

Conversation #119

What dish or meal would you like to learn how to cook?

Conversation #120

Imagine that you are a guest contestant on the latest reality cooking show, where you are asked to whip up your specialty. Thinking about everything that you know how to make, what dish do you consider your specialty?

Conversation #121

What flavor of ice cream would you gladly eat every day for an entire year?

Conversation #122

Do you use any form of social media, such as Facebook, Twitter, Instagram, etc. If so, which one is your favorite, and why?

Conversation #123

Anthony Brandt said, "Other things may change us, but we start and end with family." Describe something you love about your family.

Conversation #124

What is your least favorite or most dreaded form of exercise?

Conversation #125

If you made a New Year's Resolution today, what would your resolution be?

Conversation #126

In your opinion, what does the perfect New Year's celebration look like?

Conversation #127

Imagine you are sent to work for the circus for one year. The good news is that you can choose your act, and the circus performers will train you. What act will you be performing for the next year, and why?

Conversation #128

What future activity, vacation, or event are you most excited about right now?

Conversation #129

What video game does every adult need to play at least once in their lifetime?

Conversation #130

What is one helpful piece of advice that your parents, teacher, or a friend gave you?

Conversation #131

Animals are used to represent the four different personality types. This includes: 1. The Lion: A confidant leader, who takes charge of tasks and makes sure things get done. 2: The Otter: Outgoing, playful, and creative, the otter is the life of the party. 3. The beaver: Detail oriented and organized, the beaver is excellent at helping others stay on task. 4. The golden retriever: Warm and friendly, the golden retriever genuinely cares for others. Which personality type best describes you?

Connecting in a Disconnected World

When it comes to communicating and connecting, kids cannot afford to be average. Not only is average boring, but average does not work. If you have any doubt, consider the following statics. According to a poll of 2,000 families, the average family spends less than eight hours together each week. [4] This boils down to a mere 36 minutes on weekdays, and about five hours together over the weekend. The fact that much of this time is spent zoned out in front of the television, internet, or honed-in on cell phones, only amplifies the problem.

Studies show that Tweens, or children between the ages of 8-12, spend an average of six hours in front of a screen a day. In fact, some thirteen year olds report checking their social media accounts as much as 100 times a day.[5] With these statistics in mind, it is not surprising that face-to-face communication skills have declined.

If you purchased this book for your own home, then you have already set your family apart from the norm. If you are using this book to encourage the kids that you mentor, coach, or teach connect, then you are likely already well aware of the challenges mentioned, and know how important developing relationships is.

Now that you have reached the end of this book, the next step is to keep the conversations going. Fortunately, this can be easy. Children are continually developing and changing, so it is perfectly acceptable to return to the same conversations often. As life experiences are gained, feelings and opinions alter. Soon, fresh insights will spice up old conversations.

In short, there is simply too much connecting to do for kids and families to checkout. This is something that you almost certainly already know. However, sometimes it is helpful to have our ideas reaffirmed by someone else. The bottom line is that now that this book is complete, keep asking good questions, and keep encouraging the kids around you to connect.

Wishing you a multitude of happy conversations in the days ahead!

Sincerely,

COFFEE SHOP CONVERSATIONS

End Notes

1. Vivona Jeanine, M. *Parental Attachment Styles of Late Adolescents: Qualities of Attachment Relationships and Consequences for Adjustment,* Journal of Counseling Psychology 2000, Vol. 47, No. 3, pg 327.

2. Mehrabian Albert, *Silent Messages: Implicit Communications of Emotions and Attitudes,* Wadsworth Publishing Company, July 1972: Albert suggests that words account for 7% of communication, tone of voice 38%, and body language 55%

3. Isaacson Walter, *Steve Jobs*, Simon & Schuster, October 2011.

4. McCann Jaymi. The Daily Mail. *No time for the family? You are not alone: Parents and children spend less than an hour with each other every day because of modern demands,* July 2013. http://www.dailymail.co.uk/news/a rticle-2363193/No-time-family-You-Parents-children-spend-hour-day-

modern-
demands.html#ixzz4ZAR107Ui

5. Wallace, Kelly. CNN, *Teens spend a 'mind-boggling' 9 hours a day using media, report says.* November 3, 2013. http://www.cnn.com/2015/11/03/health/teens-tweens-media-screen-use-report/

Thumbs Up
or Thumbs Down

THANK YOU for purchasing this book!

I would love to hear from you! Your feedback not only helps me grow as a writer, it also helps to get this book into the hands of those who need it most. Online reviews are the biggest ways independent authors—like myself—connect with new readers.

If you loved the book, could you please share your experience? Leaving feedback is as easy as answering any of these questions:

- What did you enjoy about the book?
- What is your most valuable takeaway or insight?
- What have you done differently—or what will you do differently—because of what you read?
- To whom would you recommend this book?

Of course, we are looking for honest reviews. So, if you have a minute to share your experience, good or bad, please consider leaving your review!

I look forward to hearing from you!

Sincerely,
    Jed Jurchenko

About The Author

Jed Jurchenko is a husband, father to four girls, a psychology professor, and therapist. He supports passionate Christ followers in leading their families, growing their friendships, and in maturing their faith, so that they can live joy-filled, Christ-honoring lives.

Jed graduated from Southern California Seminary with a Masters of Divinity and returned to complete a second master's in psychology. In their free time, Jed and Jenny enjoy walking on the beach, reading, and spending time together as a family.

Continue the Conversation

Let's stay in touch! I always enjoy hearing what others think. Here are a number of ways to keep connected and continue the conversation:

Blog: www.CoffeeShopConversations.com

E-mail: jed@coffeeshopconversations.com

Twitter: @jjurchenko

Facebook: Coffee Shop Conversations

More Creative Conversations

Find this book and others books in the creative conversations series in Amazon.

Take your relationship from bland to inspired, passionate, and connected as you grow your insights into your partner's inner world! Whether you are newly dating or nearing your golden anniversary these conversation starters are for you! This book will help you share your heart and dive into your partner's inner world.

131 Creative Conversations for Couples

More Creative Conversations

The average family spends less than eight hours together each week. Be above average! Take your family from distant, to bonded with these value-based conversation starters.

Each chapter introduces a core virtue, followed by ten conversation starters to encourage your family to cultivate this quality. Build a multitude of happy memories as you grow, with a book the entire family will enjoy!

131 Creative Conversations for Families

54256168R00035

Made in the USA
Middletown, DE
02 December 2017